I0490063

The Comprehensive
GOAT
RAISING
GUIDE

The Secrets to Rearing Healthy
Goats for Beginners and Pros

Gabby King

CONTENTS

INTRODUCTION

Goat raising has been around for thousands of years, dating back to the earliest human civilizations. These animals were among the first to be domesticated, and for good reason. Goats are versatile animals that can provide us with milk, meat, fiber, and even companionship. They are hardy and adaptable, able to thrive in a wide range of environments and climates.

But despite their many benefits, raising goats is not without its challenges. From selecting the right breed to providing proper nutrition and healthcare, there is a lot to consider when embarking on this venture. That's why I've created "The Comprehensive Goat Raising Guide," a complete resource for anyone interested in raising goats, from beginners to experienced farmers.

This guide is designed to provide you with everything you need to know about raising goats, including information on breeds, housing, feeding, breeding, and more. We'll cover the basics of goat care, such as how to keep your goats healthy and happy, as well as more advanced topics like goat genetics and breeding programs.

If your objective is to raise goats for milk, meat, fiber, or simply as pets, this guide will help you get started. We'll explore the different breeds of goats, each with their own unique characteristics and requirements, so you can choose the right breed for your needs. We'll also provide tips on how to properly house your goats, whether you're keeping them in a backyard or on a large farm.

Feeding your goats is another important aspect of raising them, and we'll cover everything from basic nutrition to specialized diets for dairy or meat production. We'll also discuss the importance of proper healthcare, including preventative measures like vaccinations and regular checkups, as well as how to identify and treat common goat illnesses.

Breeding is another aspect of goat raising that requires careful consideration, and I'll provide you with the information you need to create a successful breeding program. We'll look at topics like selecting the right breeding stock, managing pregnancies and births, and caring for newborn kids.

At its core, "The Comprehensive Goat Raising Guide" is an exploration of these remarkable animals and the many benefits they offer. Whether you're a seasoned farmer or a curious beginner interested in raising goats for their milk, meat, or fiber, or simply want to keep them as pets, this guide will provide you with the knowledge and tools you need to succeed. So let's dive in and discover the world of goat raising together!

CHAPTER 1

GOAT RAISING:

AN OVERVIEW

The popularity of raising goats is on the rise in the United States and other parts of the world due to their hardiness and minimal care requirements. Goats make an excellent addition to homesteads or small farms, as there are many breeds available for milk, meat, and other products.

Since goats are social creatures, they thrive in herds and require companionship. While a few goats can be kept in a small area, larger herds will need more space. To keep them contained, sturdy and secure fencing is necessary as goats are known for their playful and active behavior.

A well-balanced diet is important for the health and productivity of goats. They require fresh water, quality hay or grass, and a moderate amount of grain supplemented with minerals, vitamins, and other nutrients. Researching different goat breeds is also important to find the most suitable for the desired purpose.

Vaccinations and regular deworming are essential to keep goats healthy and protected from parasites and diseases. Additionally, regular grooming including brushing, trimming hooves, and cleaning eyes and ears is necessary to maintain their overall health and cleanliness.

Goats can also be used as guard animals to protect other livestock, thanks to their strong sense of smell and alertness to danger. They can even help control weeds in pastures.

Overall, raising goats can be a rewarding experience for those who provide proper care and attention. With their low-maintenance needs, goats can be a valuable addition to any homestead or small farm, providing milk, meat, fiber, and other products to their owners.

Benefits of Raising Goats

Goats are becoming increasingly popular as a source of milk, meat, and fiber for many people. They are also a great animal to have around for companionship, and for the many benefits they provide. Here are some of the benefits of raising goats.

1. Environmentally Friendly: Goats are very environmentally friendly animals. They are browsers, meaning they prefer to eat shrubs, bushes and weeds rather than grasses. This type of diet helps keep pastures and yards free of overgrowth and weeds, saving time and money from having to mow or weed whack. Goats also require much less space than other livestock animals, such as sheep or cows.

2. Versatile: Goats are very versatile animals. They are small enough to keep in a backyard, but can also do well in larger pastures. They can be used for milk, meat, fiber, and even show animals. They are also a great way to help control weeds and overgrowth in larger pastures.

3. Low Maintenance: Goats are fairly low maintenance animals. They do not require as much care as other livestock animals, such as cows or horses. They are much easier to handle, as they are smaller and less intimidating.

4. Affordable: Goats are a very affordable option for people looking to add livestock to their farm or homestead. They require much less space and resources than other livestock animals, making them a great choice for those on a budget.

5. Companion Animals: Goats are great companion animals. They are social and can form bonds with their owners, making them a great animal to have around for companionship.

Raising goats is a great option for many people looking to add livestock to their farm or homestead. There are many benefits to raising goats, as listed above. So whether you are looking for milk, meat, fiber, or just a companion, goats are a great option and should be considered.

Different Breeds of Goats

Goats are versatile domesticated animals that are kept for a variety of purposes, including meat, milk, fiber, and even as pets. There are many different breeds of goats, each with its unique characteristics and qualities that make them suited for particular purposes.

1. **Nigerian Dwarf Goats:** Nigerian Dwarf goats are a small dairy breed that originated in West Africa. They are known for their high milk production relative to their size, and their milk has a high butterfat content, making it excellent for cheese making. Nigerian Dwarf goats are also popular as pets due to their friendly and playful nature, small size, and colorful markings. They are adaptable to a range of climates and are easy to

care for, making them a great choice for small farms and homesteads.

2. **Boer Goats:** Boer goats are a popular breed for meat production, known for their fast growth rate and large size. They have a distinctive white body with a brown head and are known for their hardiness and adaptability to different climates.

3. **Nubian Goats:** Nubian goats are a dairy breed known for their high milk production and butterfat content. They have long, floppy ears and a distinctive Roman nose. They are also known for their friendly personalities and make great pets.

4. **Alpine Goats:** Alpine goats are a hardy breed that is often kept for both milk and meat production. They are medium-sized with a wide range of colors and patterns, and they have a calm temperament, making them easy to handle.

5. **LaMancha Goats:** LaMancha goats are a dairy breed known for their high milk production and low butterfat content. They are also distinctive for their small ears, which are often referred to as

"gopher ears." They are easy to care for and have a gentle temperament.

6. **Pygmy Goats:** Pygmy goats are a miniature breed that is often kept as pets. They have a playful and curious personality and are known for their distinctive short stature and small, compact size.

7. **Saanen Goats:** Saanen goats are a dairy breed known for their high milk production and docile temperament. They are typically all-white with upright ears and a gentle disposition.

8. **Angora Goats:** Angora goats are a fiber breed that is primarily kept for their luxurious mohair fleece. They have a distinctive long, curly coat and are often shorn twice a year to harvest their fiber.

9. **Cashmere Goats:** Cashmere goats are another fiber breed known for their soft, fine undercoat. They are typically smaller than Angora goats and are often crossbred with other breeds to improve their fiber quality.

10. **Kiko Goats:** Kiko goats are a meat breed that is known for their hardiness and adaptability. They have a distinctive brown coat and are often raised on range land, making them a popular choice for sustainable meat production.

11. **Spanish Goats:** Spanish goats are a hardy breed that is often raised for meat production. They have a distinctive range of colors and patterns and are known for their adaptability to harsh environments.

The preceding are some of the different breeds of goats, each with its unique characteristics and qualities that make them suited for particular purposes.

Understanding Goat Behavior

Goats are social and intelligent animals that are widely domesticated for meat, milk, and fiber production. They are found all over the world, from the mountains of Asia and Europe to the grasslands of Africa and the Americas. Understanding goat behavior is important for proper care and management of these animals.

Goats are herd animals, and thrive in groups. They are social creatures and enjoy the company of other goats. Goats establish a hierarchy within their herds, and there is always a dominant goat that leads the group. The dominant goat is usually the strongest and most aggressive in the group, and it gets the best food, water, and shelter. The other goats in the herd follow the dominant goat and respect its authority.

Goats are curious animals and are always exploring their surroundings. They are intelligent animals and can learn quickly. They are also known for their playful nature, and they enjoy playing with objects such as balls, ropes, and other toys. They are very active animals, and they require plenty of space to move around and exercise. Goats love to climb and jump, and they are very good at it.

Goats are browsers, and they prefer to eat leaves, twigs, and other plant material rather than grass. They have a very sensitive sense of smell and taste, and they are very picky eaters. They will often sniff their food before eating it, and if they don't like the smell or taste, they will refuse to eat it. Goats also require plenty of water, and they will drink about 1-2 gallons of water per day.

Goats are very vocal animals, and they communicate with each other through a variety of sounds such as bleats, moans, and grunts. They also use body language to communicate, such as lowering their head and raising their tail when they are scared or threatened. Goats can be trained to respond to voice commands, and they can learn to come when called and to follow certain routines.

Goats are also known for their stubbornness. You might have heard the saying, "as stubborn as a goat". They can be very difficult to train, and they can become very attached to their routines and habits. They can also become very aggressive if they feel threatened or if they perceive a challenge to their dominance. It is imperative to establish a good relationship with goats and to be patient and gentle with them.

Goats are also very adaptable animals, and they can live in a variety of environments, from the hot deserts of Africa to the cold mountains of Asia. They are very hardy animals, and they can survive on very little food and water.

Understanding goat behavior is essential for proper care and management of these animals. Proper care and management are essential to keep goats healthy and productive, and to ensure their well-being.

CHAPTER 2

SETTING UP YOUR GOAT FARM

Goat farming has become a popular and lucrative enterprise for many farmers around the world. As mentioned earlier, goats are easy to manage, adaptable to different climates, and can provide a range of products including meat, milk, and fiber. However, starting a goat farm requires careful planning and attention to detail. In this chapter, we will cover the basic steps involved in setting up a successful goat farm.

Research and planning: Before starting a goat farm, it is essential to conduct thorough research and planning. This involves identifying the market demand for goat products in your area, determining the breed of goats to raise, and creating a business plan. You should also consider the necessary equipment and facilities, as well as the cost and availability of feed and other supplies.

Selecting the breed of goats: There are many different breeds of goats, each with their own unique characteristics and purposes. Some breeds are raised primarily for meat production, while others are kept for milk or fiber. When selecting a breed, it is important to consider factors such as climate, terrain, and market demand. Popular meat breeds include Boer, Kiko, and Spanish goats, while popular milk breeds include Saanen, Alpine, and Nubian goats.

Building facilities: Goats require adequate housing and fencing to ensure their safety and comfort. A good goat shelter should provide protection from the elements, adequate ventilation, and space for goats to move around freely. Fencing is also handy in keeping goats contained and safe from predators. The type of fencing required will depend on the terrain and the size and breed of goats being raised.

Providing adequate nutrition: Goats require a balanced diet to maintain good health and productivity. This includes a combination of hay, pasture, and commercial feed. The specific requirements will vary depending on the breed, age, and reproductive status of the goats. It is important to work with a veterinarian or animal nutritionist to develop a feeding program that meets the needs of your goats.

Establishing a breeding program: If your goal is to produce goat milk or meat, you will need to establish a breeding program. This involves selecting high-quality breeding stock and developing a breeding plan to ensure the genetic diversity and health of your herd. It is important to work with a veterinarian or animal breeder to establish a breeding program that meets your goals.

Developing a marketing strategy: Once you have established a goat farm and have products to sell, you will need to develop a marketing strategy. This may include advertising your products through social media, attending farmer's markets, or establishing relationships with local restaurants and grocery stores. It is important to understand the market demand for your products and to develop a pricing strategy that is competitive and profitable.

There's no doubt that setting up a goat farm requires careful planning, research, and attention to detail. By selecting the right breed of goats, providing adequate nutrition and housing, establishing a breeding program, and developing a marketing strategy, you can build a successful and profitable goat farm. With patience and hard work, you can create a sustainable business that provides high-quality goat products to your community.

Selecting the Right Location

Selecting the right location is a crucial aspect of goat raising, as it can have a significant impact on the health, well-being, and productivity of your goats. Before you start raising goats, you need to carefully evaluate your potential location and ensure that it meets the needs of your animals.

One of the primary considerations when selecting a location for goat raising is the availability of suitable grazing land. Goats are natural browsers and require access to a variety of vegetation to meet their nutritional needs. Ideally, your location should provide access to pasture, woodland, or scrubland where your goats can browse freely. The quality and quantity of forage available will depend on the climate, soil type, and vegetation in your area, so it is important to research these factors carefully.

Another key consideration is the availability of water. Goats require clean, fresh water at all times, and you will need to ensure that your location provides a reliable source of water. This could include a natural stream or river, a well, or a rainwater catchment system. You should also ensure that your location is not prone to flooding or waterlogging, as this can create health problems for your goats.

The climate of your location is also a key thing to consider. Goats are adaptable animals, but they do best in moderate temperatures and a dry climate. Extreme heat or cold can be stressful for goats and increase their risk of disease. If you live in an area with very hot or very cold temperatures, you may need to provide additional shelter or climate control measures to ensure the health of your animals.

In addition to the natural environment, you should also consider the availability of veterinary care and other support services in your area. Goats are prone to a range of health issues, and it is essential to have access to a qualified veterinarian who can provide regular check-ups and emergency care when needed. You may also need to access support services such as feed suppliers, equipment rentals, or breeding programs, so it is important to ensure that these are available in your area.

Finally, you should consider the legal requirements and zoning regulations in your area. Many municipalities have regulations regarding the number of animals that can be kept on a property, as well as rules regarding housing and fencing requirements. Before you start raising goats, do well to research these regulations and ensure that you are in compliance.

Building Goat Shelters and Fencing

Building goat shelters and fencing is a necessary aspect of keeping goats, whether for meat, milk, or as pets. Goats need a safe and comfortable place to live, and a well-built shelter and sturdy fencing can provide them with the protection they need.

When it comes to building goat shelters, there are several factors to consider. The first thing to consider is the size of the shelter. The size of the shelter will depend on the number of goats you have and the breed of goats. Goats need enough space to move around, so the shelter should be large enough to accommodate them comfortably. As a general rule, you should allow at least 10 to 12 square feet of space per goat.

Another important factor to consider when building a goat shelter is the type of material to use. The most common materials used for goat shelters include wood, metal, and plastic. Each material has its advantages and disadvantages, so choose the material that will work best for your particular situation.

Wood is a popular choice for goat shelters because it is easy to work with and provides good insulation. However, wood can also be expensive and requires regular maintenance to prevent rot and decay.

Metal is a durable and long-lasting material that can provide excellent protection from the elements. However, metal can be noisy during heavy rain or hail, which can be a source of stress for some goats.

Plastic is an affordable option that is easy to clean and maintain. However, plastic can be prone to cracking or breaking over time, which can compromise its effectiveness as a shelter.

When building a goat shelter, make sure you provide adequate ventilation to keep the air fresh and prevent the buildup of moisture. Proper ventilation can also help regulate the temperature inside the shelter, keeping goats comfortable in both hot and cold weather.

Once you have built a shelter for your goats, you will also need to install fencing to keep them safe and contained. Fencing is important for several reasons, including keeping predators out and preventing goats from wandering off.

There are several types of fencing that can be used for goats, including woven wire, electric, and chain link. The type of fencing you choose will depend on your budget, the size of your property, and the level of protection you need.

Woven wire is a popular choice for goat fencing because it is durable and can keep predators out. However, woven wire can be expensive and difficult to install.

Electric fencing is an affordable option that can be effective at keeping goats contained. However, electric fencing requires regular maintenance to ensure it is working properly.

Chain link fencing is a durable and long-lasting option that can provide excellent protection for goats. However, chain link fencing can be expensive and may not be as effective at keeping predators out as other types of fencing.

When installing fencing for goats, make sure the fence is sturdy and secure. Goats are notorious for testing boundaries, so the fence should be able to withstand their pushing and climbing.

Remember, a well-built shelter and sturdy fencing can provide goats with the protection they need to stay safe and healthy. When building a shelter or installing fencing, it's important to consider the size of your goats, the materials you will use, and the type of fencing that will work best for your situation. With the right shelter and fencing, your goats will be happy and healthy for years to come.

Choosing the Right Equipment and Tools

As a goat raiser, one of the most important things you can do is choose the right equipment and tools for the job. From fencing and housing to feeding and milking, the right equipment can make all the difference in the health and well-being of your goats, as well as your own efficiency and productivity as a farmer.

One of the first things you will need to consider is your fencing. Goats are notorious for their ability to escape, so it is required that you choose a fencing system that is secure and reliable. Some options include woven wire, electric fencing, and welded wire panels. Each has its own benefits and drawbacks, so it is important to research each option thoroughly and choose the one that best fits your needs and budget.

Once you have your fencing in place, you will need to consider your housing. Goats require shelter from the elements, as well as a place to sleep and rest. The type of housing you choose will depend on a number of factors, including the number of goats you have, the climate in your area, and your budget. Some options include a simple three-sided shelter, a barn with stalls, or a hoop house.

Next, you will need to consider your feeding equipment. Goats require a balanced diet that includes hay, grain, and fresh water. Depending on the size of your operation, you may need to invest in equipment such as a hay feeder, grain feeder, and water troughs. You may also want to consider a mineral feeder to ensure your goats have access to essential minerals and vitamins.

Milking equipment is another key consideration for those raising dairy goats. Milking by hand is an option, but it can be time-consuming and tiring. Milking machines are available in a range of sizes and styles, so it is important to choose one that is appropriate for your herd size and milking needs. You will also need to invest in supplies such as milk buckets, filters, and teat dip.

Other tools and equipment that may be useful for goat raisers include hoof trimmers, clippers, and de-wormers. Hoof trimmers are used to keep goats' hooves healthy and free from overgrowth, while clippers are used to shear goats for showing or to prevent overheating in hot weather. De-wormers are essential to keep your goats healthy and free from parasites.

When choosing equipment and tools for goat raising, you should consider not only the initial cost but also the long-term costs associated with maintenance and replacement. It may be tempting to choose cheaper equipment to save money, but this can often result in more costly repairs and replacements down the road.

Having mentioned choosing the right equipment, it is also important to use it properly and maintain it regularly. This includes cleaning and sanitizing equipment after each use, checking for damage or wear and tear, and storing equipment properly when not in use.

CHAPTER 3

FEEDING YOUR GOATS

Goats are a great animal to have on any farm, and they can provide milk, meat, and even fiber for clothing and other products. However, goats require a special diet to stay healthy and happy. Proper feeding is essential for the health and well-being of your goats and can make all the difference in their productivity.

Generally, as grazers, goats prefer to browse and eat a variety of plant materials such as weeds and shrubs. They also need a source of hay or forage, such as alfalfa or grass, in their diet. Hay should be stored in a dry area, free from moisture and pests. Hay should be free of mold and dust, and should be stored in a location that is protected from the elements.

Goats also need a source of grain, such as oats, corn, or barley. They can also benefit from access to a mineral supplement, such as a block made specifically for goats. A mineral supplement should contain calcium, magnesium, phosphorus, and other vitamins and minerals. Goats need to be fed a balanced diet, and it's essential to ensure the proper ratio of grain to hay in their diet.

In addition to hay and grain, goats also need access to fresh, clean water. Water should be available at all times and should be changed regularly.

They should be monitored to ensure they are receiving the proper amount of feed. A goat's appetite can vary due to the weather, health, and age. If a goat is not eating as much as they should, they may need to be supplemented with additional feed.

Goats should also be dewormed regularly, as parasites can affect their health and digestion, and also be vaccinated against certain diseases.

In a nutshell, proper feeding is essential for the health and well-being of your goats. It's imperative that you provide them with a balanced diet, including hay, grain, a mineral supplement, and fresh water. Don't forget to monitor your goats to ensure they are receiving the proper amount of feed, and take the necessary steps to prevent parasites and disease. With the right care and nutrition, your goats can remain healthy and productive.

Nutritional Requirements for Goats

Goats are ruminant animals, which means they require a specific diet to support their digestive system and overall health. Proper nutrition is essential for the growth, reproduction, and maintenance of goats, as well as for their milk or meat production. In this section, we will discuss the nutritional requirements for goats, including their dietary needs, feeding management, and common feeding practices.

Dietary Needs

Goats require a balanced diet that includes six essential nutrients: **carbohydrates**, **proteins**, **fats**, **vitamins**, **minerals**, and **water**. Each of these nutrients plays a vital role in the overall health of goats and must be provided in adequate amounts. Here is a breakdown of each nutrient and its function in goat nutrition:

1. Carbohydrates: Carbohydrates provide energy to goats and are the main source of calories in their diet. Good sources of carbohydrates for goats include grains, hay, and grass.

2. Proteins: Proteins are essential for muscle growth and repair, as well as for the production of milk and wool. Good sources of protein for goats

include alfalfa, clover, soybean meal, and cottonseed meal.

3. Fats: Fats provide energy to goats and are necessary for the absorption of fat-soluble vitamins. Good sources of fat for goats include vegetable oil and animal fat.

4. Vitamins: Vitamins are essential for various functions in goats, including metabolism and immunity. Goats require both fat-soluble and water-soluble vitamins, such as vitamin A, D, E, K, and B-complex vitamins.

5. Minerals: Minerals are essential for bone development, muscle contraction, and overall health. Good sources of minerals for goats include salt, calcium, phosphorus, and copper.

6. Water: Water is essential for hydration and proper digestion in goats. Goats should have access to clean, fresh water at all times.

Feeding Management

Feeding management is an important aspect of goat nutrition. Goats should be fed a balanced diet that meets their nutritional requirements, and their feeding schedule should be consistent. Here are some feeding management practices to consider:

a. **Feed quality:** Goats require high-quality feed that is free from mold and other contaminants. Hay should be green, leafy, and free from dust and mold.

b. **Feed quantity:** Goats should be fed according to their weight, age, and production level. As a general rule, goats should consume about 3-4% of their body weight in dry matter per day.

c. **Feeding schedule:** Goats should be fed at regular intervals to maintain a healthy digestive system. Adult goats should be fed twice a day, while young goats may require more frequent feedings.

d. **Supplements:** Goats may require supplements to meet their nutritional needs, especially during certain stages of life, such as pregnancy or lactation. Supplements should be added to the diet in consultation with a veterinarian or animal nutritionist.

Common Feeding Practices

There are several common feeding practices for goats that can help meet their nutritional requirements. These include:

1. Forage: Goats require forage in their diet, such as hay or pasture. Forage provides fiber, which is essential for proper digestion and can prevent digestive problems such as bloat.

2. Grain: Grain can be fed to goats as a supplement to their forage diet. Grain provides energy and protein, but it should be fed in moderation, as overfeeding can lead to digestive problems.

3. <u>Minerals:</u> Goats require minerals in their diet, such as salt, calcium, and phosphorus. Mineral supplements can be added to their diet to ensure adequate intake.

By providing a balanced diet and proper feeding management, goats can thrive and maintain optimal health. It is paramount to consult with a veterinarian or animal nutritionist to ensure that the nutritional requirements of goats are met based on their age, weight, and production level.

Different Types of Feed

As a goat raiser, you need to understand the different types of feed available for your animals. Feeding your goats the right type of feed is essential for their health and wellbeing, and can even impact the quality of the milk and meat they produce. Now, let's explore the different types of feed that are commonly used in goat raising.

Hay

Hay is one of the most commonly used types of feed for goats. It is made from dried grass, legumes, or other plants, and is typically harvested during the summer months. Hay is a good source of fiber, which is needed for maintaining healthy digestion in goats. It also contains protein, vitamins, and minerals that goats need for optimal health.

There are different types of hay, including alfalfa, timothy, and grass hay. Alfalfa hay is high in protein, making it a good choice for goats that are pregnant or lactating. Timothy hay is lower in protein but high in fiber, making it a good choice for goats that need to maintain their weight. Grass hay is also high in fiber, and is a good choice for goats that are grazing on pasture but need additional forage.

Grain

Grain is another type of feed that is commonly used in goat raising. It is high in energy and protein, making it a good choice for goats that need to gain weight or produce milk. However, it is important to feed grain in moderation, as too much can lead to digestive issues and even death.

Different types of grain that can be fed to goats include corn, oats, and barley. Corn is high in energy but low in protein, making it a good choice for goats that need to gain weight. Oats are high in protein and fiber, making them a good choice for lactating goats. Barley is also high in energy, and can be fed to goats that need to gain weight or produce milk.

Silage

Silage is a type of feed that is made from fermented grass or other plants. It is typically stored in a silo, and can be fed to goats throughout the year. Silage is a good source of energy and protein, and can help goats maintain their weight and produce milk.

However, ensure that the silage is properly fermented and stored, as improperly fermented silage can be harmful to goats. It is also necessary to feed silage in moderation, as too much can lead to digestive issues.

Forage

Forage is any type of plant material that goats can graze on. It can include grass, weeds, and other plants that are found in pastures and fields. Forage is a good source of fiber, which is important for maintaining healthy digestion in goats.

However, it is crucial to ensure that the forage is of good quality, as poor quality forage can lead to digestive issues and even death. You also need to ascertain that the forage is free of toxic plants, as some plants can be harmful to goats.

Supplements

Supplements are a type of feed that can be used to provide goats with additional nutrients that they may be lacking in their diet. Supplements can include minerals, vitamins, and other nutrients that are meant for maintaining optimal health in goats.

However, supplements should be fed in moderation, as too much can lead to health issues. It is also essential to ensure that the supplements are appropriate for goats, as some supplements that are designed for other animals may not be suitable for goats.

Goat farming allows the use of a variety of feeds, including hay, grain, silage, forage, and supplements. Based on your goats' age, weight, health, and nutritional requirements, it's critical to pick the correct kind of feed for them. To avoid health problems in your goats, it's also crucial to make sure the feed is of excellent quality and given in moderation. The health and production of your goats can be increased by feeding them a well-balanced diet that contains a range of feeds.

Feeding Schedule and Quantity

When it comes to raising goats, one of the most important aspects to consider is their feeding schedule and the quantity of feed they receive. Proper nutrition is crucial to the health and well-being of your goats, and it can impact their growth, milk production, and overall performance.

The feeding schedule for goats depends on their age and stage of development. Newborn kids should be fed colostrum within the first few hours of life, which contains essential antibodies to protect them from diseases. After that, they should be fed milk from their mother or a milk replacer every 2-3 hours for the first week of life. As they grow older, the frequency of feeding can be gradually reduced to 3-4 times a day, and then to twice a day until they are weaned.

Adult goats should be fed twice a day, in the morning and evening. They should have access to fresh water at all times, as well as hay or pasture. The amount of feed they need depends on their body weight, age, and activity level. As a general rule, goats should consume 2-4% of their body weight in feed per day. For example, a 100-pound goat would require 2-4 pounds of feed per day.

The type of feed your goats need will also vary depending on their age and purpose. For example, growing kids and lactating does require more protein and energy than adult males or non-lactating females. Good quality hay is a staple in a goat's diet, but it is not enough to meet their nutritional needs alone. Goats also need a balanced diet of grains, such as corn, barley, or oats, and protein sources, such as soybean meal, alfalfa pellets, or dried distillers grains.

It is essential to provide your goats with a balanced diet and to avoid overfeeding or underfeeding them. Overfeeding can lead to health problems such as obesity, while underfeeding can lead to malnutrition, stunted growth, and decreased milk production. Regular weighing of your goats can help you adjust their feeding schedule and quantity accordingly.

Apart from their regular feed, goats also need access to minerals and vitamins. A mineral block or loose minerals can be provided free-choice to goats, and it should contain essential minerals such as calcium, phosphorus, and salt. Vitamin supplements can also be added to their diet if needed.

When feeding your goats, endeavor to keep their environment clean and free from moldy or spoiled feed. Goats are susceptible to digestive issues and can suffer from bloat or diarrhea if they eat contaminated feed. Their feeders and waterers should be cleaned regularly, and any leftover feed should be removed promptly.

By following these guidelines, you can ensure that your goats thrive and perform to their full potential.

CHAPTER 4

HEALTH AND HYGIENE

Health and Hygiene is an critical topic when it comes to raising goats. Goats are quite susceptible to disease and parasites, so preventive measures should be taken to protect your goats from harm. Good health and hygiene practices are a must when it comes to keeping your goats healthy and happy.

The first step in protecting your goat's health is making sure that their environment is clean and free of potential contaminants. This includes cleaning out the goat's pen and providing clean bedding on a regular basis. It's also important to give your goats a safe space away from potential predators.

In addition to the environment, goats need a healthy diet in order to stay healthy. Providing a balanced diet of hay, grains, and fresh vegetables is essential to keep your goats healthy. Goats also need to have access to plenty of fresh, clean water.

Regular veterinary care is also a crucial part of keeping your goats healthy. Regular check-ups with a veterinarian can help nip in the bud any potential health problems before they become serious. Vaccinations are also necessary in order to protect your goats from diseases.

Grooming your goats is another important part of keeping them healthy. Brushing and trimming hooves can help reduce the risk of infection and other illnesses. Regularly checking for parasites, such as lice and mites, can also prevent the spread of these parasites to other animals.

It's imperative to practice biosecurity measures when it comes to raising goats. This includes washing hands after handling any animals, keeping the goat's pen separate from other animals, and not sharing any equipment between animals. Biosecurity measures can help ensure that your goats stay healthy and free from disease.

Preventing Common Goat Diseases

Keeping goats can be a rewarding and fulfilling experience, but it also comes with the responsibility of ensuring their health and well-being. Just like any other animal, goats can fall ill and suffer from various diseases if not properly taken care of. Here are some tips on preventing common goat diseases to keep your goats healthy and happy.

First and foremost, it's essential to provide your goats with a clean and safe living environment. Make sure their living area is well-ventilated, free of dampness, and has adequate space for them to move around. A dirty and unhygienic living space can lead to the growth of harmful bacteria and parasites that can cause various diseases. Keep their bedding clean and dry, and remove any manure or urine regularly.

One of the most critical aspects of preventing goat diseases is proper nutrition. Provide your goats with a balanced and varied diet, depending on their age, weight, and breed. Goats are herbivores, so their diet should consist of mostly hay and grass, supplemented with grains, minerals, and vitamins. Make sure they have access to clean water at all times, as dehydration can lead to various health problems.

Another way to prevent goat diseases is to maintain proper hygiene practices. Wash your hands thoroughly before and after handling your goats, and wear protective clothing and gloves when necessary. Keep their hooves trimmed and clean to prevent foot rot, which is a common problem among goats. Regularly check their ears, eyes, and nose for any signs of infection, and consult with a veterinarian if necessary.

In this scenario, Vaccinations are also crucial in preventing goat diseases. Consult with a veterinarian to determine which vaccines your goats need, based on their age, breed, and environment. Common vaccines include those for tetanus, rabies, and pneumonia. Administer the vaccines according to the recommended schedule, and keep accurate records of your goats' vaccinations.

Parasites can also cause various diseases in goats. Common parasites include worms, lice, and mites. Regularly deworm your goats and treat them for external parasites as needed. Consult with a veterinarian to determine the appropriate deworming and parasite treatment schedule for your goats.

Lastly, it's essential to observe your goats regularly and watch for any signs of illness. Goats are prey animals, so they tend to hide signs of illness until they become severe. Some common signs of illness include loss of appetite, lethargy, coughing, diarrhea, and fever. If you notice any of these symptoms, consult with a veterinarian immediately.

Vaccination Schedule

As a goat raiser, please ensure that your animals are healthy and protected from diseases. One of the best ways to achieve this is through vaccination. Vaccines work by stimulating the immune system of the animal to produce an immune response that will protect them from specific diseases.

When it comes to goat vaccination, there are several factors to consider, including the age of the animal, the type of vaccine, and the timing of the vaccination. It is important to follow a vaccination schedule to ensure that your goats receive the necessary vaccines at the right time.

The first vaccine that a goat will receive is usually the CD&T vaccine, which protects against clostridium perfringens type C and D as well as tetanus. This vaccine is typically administered to kids at around 8-10 weeks of age. It is imperative to follow up with a booster shot 4-6 weeks later to ensure maximum protection.

Another important vaccine for goats is the rabies vaccine. Rabies is a deadly disease that can affect both animals and humans. Goats are at risk of contracting rabies through bites from infected animals such as skunks, raccoons, and bats. It is recommended to vaccinate goats against rabies at around 3-4 months of age, followed by annual boosters.

Other vaccines that may be necessary depending on your location and specific herd health concerns include the pneumonia vaccine, the Johne's vaccine, and the caseous lymphadenitis vaccine. Your veterinarian can help you determine which vaccines are necessary for your goats based on your location and herd health concerns.

Note that vaccines can only do so much to protect your goats from diseases. Proper management practices such as keeping the environment clean, providing good nutrition, and minimizing stress can also go a long way in keeping your goats healthy.

Also ensure you keep records of all vaccinations administered to your goats. This can help you keep track of when each vaccine was given, which vaccines may need boosters, and can also be useful if you ever need to provide proof of vaccination.

Maintaining Cleanliness and Hygiene

Maintaining cleanliness and hygiene is an essential aspect of raising goats, and it plays a significant role in keeping them healthy and disease-free. As a goat owner, you need to create and maintain a clean and hygienic environment for your goats, both inside and outside their living space. Here are some tips on how to maintain cleanliness and hygiene in your goat raising operation.

First and foremost, it is essential to keep your goat's living space clean and well-maintained. Goats are naturally clean animals, and they prefer living in a clean and dry environment. Their living space should be free from any accumulated manure, urine, or other waste. This not only helps to prevent the spread of diseases but also keeps your goats comfortable and happy.

To maintain a clean living space, you should have proper drainage and ventilation systems in place. Ensure that there is proper airflow in the barn or shelter, and that the bedding is regularly cleaned and replaced. The bedding material should be dry and absorbent, and changed regularly to prevent the accumulation of moisture.

Regular cleaning of the goat's living space is also important. This involves removing any debris, such as hay or straw, and sweeping the floors. You can also use a disinfectant to clean the floors and walls to prevent the growth and spread of harmful bacteria.

In addition to the living space, always ensure you maintain hygiene when handling your goats. This includes washing your hands before and after handling the goats, as well as using clean and sanitized equipment. Also keep your goats' hooves trimmed and clean to prevent the buildup of dirt and bacteria.

Feeding your goats clean and fresh food and water is another prudent measure to take in order to maintain their overall hygiene and health. Ensure that their feeders and waterers are regularly cleaned and sanitized, and that they are not sharing their food or water with other animals.

You also have to factor in regular veterinary checkups, to maintain your goats' hygiene and health. This includes deworming and vaccinating your goats as recommended by your veterinarian.

This helps to prevent the spread of diseases and parasites among your goats.

Don't forget to keep an eye out for any signs of illness or disease in your goats. This includes monitoring their behavior, appetite, and general appearance. If you notice any unusual symptoms, don't hesitate to consult with your veterinarian immediately.

CHAPTER 5

BREEDING AND REPRODUCTION

Breeding and Reproduction are key aspects of raising goats. It is not only important to select the right goats for breeding, but also to understand the reproductive cycle and how to manage the goats during breeding and birthing.

Goats are seasonal breeders, which means they will only breed during certain times of the year. For goats, the breeding season usually falls between late fall and early spring. During the breeding season, goats will come into heat and the females will be ready to mate. The male goat will usually display some behaviors, such as mounting the female, to indicate he is ready to breed.

Once the female is bred, she will go through a gestation period of approximately five months before giving birth to her kids. During this time, you should provide her with the proper nutrition and care to ensure she remains healthy and is able to produce healthy kids.

Once the female gives birth, the newborn kids will require a lot of attention and care. This includes regular feeding, proper sanitation, and socialization. It is also important to provide the kids with the necessary vaccinations to protect them from disease.

When the kids reach the appropriate age, they can be bred. The female kids should not be bred until they are at least a year old and the male kids should not be bred until they are at least two years old. It is also vital to ensure that the kids are of the same breed and have the same bloodlines in order to produce healthy offspring.

Everyone who rears goats should understand the risks associated with the practice. Some of these risks include diseases, birth defects, and infertility. You need to be aware of these risks and take the necessary precautions to protect the goats and their offspring.

Understanding Goat Reproduction

Goat reproduction is a complex process that involves several stages and factors. Understanding goat reproduction is important for breeders and farmers who want to optimize breeding programs, improve herd management, and ensure the production of healthy offspring. In this section, I will provide a comprehensive overview of goat reproduction, including the anatomy and physiology of goats, the breeding cycle, and factors that affect reproductive performance.

Anatomy and Physiology of Goats

To understand goat reproduction, you first need to understand the anatomy and physiology of goats. Goats are mammals and have a reproductive system that is similar to other mammals. Female goats, also known as does, have two ovaries and a uterus, while male goats, also known as bucks, have two testicles and a penis. The reproductive organs of goats are located in the pelvic cavity, which is situated between the hind legs.

The Breeding Cycle

The breeding cycle of goats can vary depending on several factors such as breed, age, and environmental conditions. Female goats typically reach sexual maturity between 5-12 months of age, while male goats reach sexual maturity at around 6-12 months of age. The breeding season for goats is typically from August to January, with the peak season occurring between September to November. However, some breeds of goats can breed throughout the year.

The estrous cycle of female goats lasts for approximately 21 days, during which they are receptive to mating. The estrous cycle is divided into four phases: proestrus, estrus, metestrus, and diestrus. The proestrus phase is characterized by the development of follicles in the ovaries and an increase in estrogen levels. The estrus phase is the period when the female is receptive to the male and ovulation occurs. The metestrus phase is a period of luteal formation, while the diestrus phase is the period of luteal regression.

Factors Affecting Reproductive Performance

Several factors can affect the reproductive performance of goats. Nutrition is one of the most key factors that influence reproductive performance. A balanced diet that includes the appropriate amounts of protein, minerals, and vitamins is essential for optimal reproductive performance. Poor nutrition can result in delayed puberty, decreased fertility, and reduced milk production.

Environmental conditions can also affect reproductive performance. Goats require a comfortable and stress-free environment to reproduce successfully. High temperatures, humidity, and exposure to harsh weather conditions can adversely affect reproductive performance.

Disease and parasites can also affect reproductive performance. It is important to ensure that goats are vaccinated against diseases such as brucellosis and that they are regularly dewormed to prevent parasitic infections.

The reproduction of goats is a multi-stage, multi-factor process. Breeders and farmers who wish to optimize breeding programs and enhance herd management must have a thorough understanding of the anatomy and physiology of goats, the breeding cycle, and the variables that impact reproductive success. A balanced food, a cozy habitat, and suitable medical treatment can all assist to promote effective reproduction and the birth of healthy young in goats.

Selecting the Right Breeding Stock

Breeding is a vital aspect of goat raising, and selecting the right breeding stock is crucial to ensure the success of the breeding program. The selection process involves evaluating various factors, including physical characteristics, genetic potential, and health status.

Physical Characteristics

When selecting breeding stock, physical characteristics should be taken into consideration. The animal's conformation and body structure should be evaluated, including the shape of the head, neck, and body. Look for animals that have a good overall appearance and are free from defects such as crooked legs or other abnormalities.

The animal's size should also be considered. Breed standards typically exist for goats, and the ideal size for each breed should be taken into account. Larger goats may produce more milk or meat, but smaller goats may be easier to handle and require less feed.

Genetic Potential

Genetic potential is another critical factor to consider when selecting breeding stock. The animal's pedigree and lineage should be examined to determine its genetic traits. Pedigree information can provide insight into an animal's strengths and weaknesses, as well as the traits it is likely to pass on to its offspring.

Genetic testing is also becoming increasingly popular in goat breeding. These tests can provide valuable information about an animal's genetic makeup, including its susceptibility to certain diseases and its potential for producing high-quality milk or meat.

Health Status

The health of the breeding stock is crucial to the success of the breeding program. Look for animals that are free from any diseases or health issues.

The animal's history of health problems should be examined, including any previous treatments or medications. Any history of disease in the animal's lineage should also be taken into consideration.

Besides physical examinations, regular veterinary check-ups and testing should be performed to ensure the animal's ongoing health. Vaccinations and other preventative measures should be taken to keep the animal free from disease.

Breeding Goals

Before selecting breeding stock, you need have clear breeding goals in mind. The goals of the breeding program should be aligned with the breed standards and the intended use of the offspring. For example, if the goal is to produce dairy goats, then selecting animals with high milk production potential should be a priority.

Breeding Programs

Breeding programs can be designed to achieve different goals, and the selection of breeding stock should be based on these goals. Programs can be designed to improve specific traits, such as milk production or meat quality, or to maintain breed standards.

It is important to keep detailed records of breeding outcomes and to evaluate the success of the program regularly. This will allow for adjustments to be made and for the program to be fine-tuned over time.

In sum, selecting the right breeding stock is crucial for the success of a goat breeding program. Physical characteristics, genetic potential, and health status should all be taken into consideration when choosing breeding animals. Breeding goals should be clearly defined, and programs should be designed to achieve these goals. Regular evaluation and adjustment of the breeding program will help ensure its ongoing success.

Caring for Pregnant Goats and Kids

Caring for pregnant goats and their kids is an indispensable aspect of goat farming. As a goat farmer, it's crucial to take good care of your pregnant goats and their offspring to ensure their health and wellbeing. Here, we will look at some tips and guidelines to help you provide the best care for your pregnant goats and their kids.

Firstly, it's important to make sure that your pregnant goats are in good health before they give birth. You should provide them with a balanced diet that includes hay, fresh water, and a mineral block. You can also supplement their diet with grain or pellets to ensure that they're getting all the nutrients they need. Additionally, you should make sure that they're vaccinated and dewormed to prevent any diseases or infections.

As your goats approach their due date, do well to provide them with a clean and comfortable birthing area. This area should be warm, dry, and free from drafts. You can use straw or shavings as bedding to keep them comfortable. You should also make sure that the area is easily accessible so that you can assist with the birthing process if necessary.

When your goats give birth, monitor them closely to make sure that they're nursing their kids properly. You should check the kids' weight regularly to make sure that they're gaining weight and growing properly. If you notice that a kid isn't nursing well or isn't gaining weight, you may need to intervene and bottle-feed them.

In addition to providing proper nutrition and monitoring their health, you should also make sure that your goats and their kids have access to clean water at all times. You should change their water frequently to ensure that it's fresh and free from contaminants.

As the kids grow, see to it that you to provide them with a safe and secure area to play and explore. You should make sure that the area is free from any hazards, such as sharp objects or toxic plants. You should also provide them with plenty of fresh hay or forage to help them develop strong digestive systems.

When it comes time to wean the kids, you should do so gradually to minimize stress and ensure a smooth transition. You can start by separating them from their mothers for short periods of time and gradually increase the length of time as they adjust. During this time, you should provide them with a high-quality diet to support their growth and development.

Caring for pregnant goats and their kids requires attention to detail and a commitment to providing the best possible care. By providing a balanced diet, monitoring their health, and creating a safe and comfortable environment, you can help ensure the health and wellbeing of your goats and their offspring.

CHAPTER 6

MILKING GOATS

Goat milking is the process of extracting milk from a goat for human consumption. It is a practice that has been around for thousands of years, and is still popular today for many reasons. Goats are small and relatively easy to care for, and their milk is rich and nutritious. In some cases, goat milk can even be used as a substitute for cow's milk.

The process of milking a goat is fairly straightforward. You first need to make sure that the goat is well-fed and calm. You can then place the goat in a milking stand or box, with its head and neck secured. This will make it easier to handle and keep the goat comfortable during the milking process. Once the goat is secured in the milking stand, you can then use a milking machine, or do it by hand. If you do it by hand, you should use a clean, sterilized bucket and a milking cup.

When milking the goat, you have to be gentle and make sure that you are using clean, sanitized equipment. If you are using a milking machine, make sure to clean it regularly to avoid contamination. Also ensure that the temperature of the milk is kept below 40 degrees Fahrenheit to avoid spoilage.

When milking the goat, you should get a good amount of milk in each session. A good milking session will yield about two to three quarts of milk. Depending on the size of the goat, you may be able to get more milk in a single session.

After milking the goat, it is important to store the milk properly. It should be refrigerated immediately, and kept at a temperature below 40 degrees Fahrenheit. If you plan to freeze the milk, make sure to cool it to below 40 degrees Fahrenheit first. This will prevent bacteria from growing in the milk.

As one who rears goats, goat milking can be a rewarding experience for you. You need to be aware of the proper techniques to ensure that the milk is safe and of good quality. With the right knowledge and care, you can enjoy fresh goat milk that is both delicious and nutritious.

Milking Techniques

Milking goats is a vital part of goat raising, whether for personal use or for commercial purposes. As a goat farmer, it's essential to learn the right milking techniques to ensure the health and productivity of your goats, as well as the quality of the milk you produce.

Before diving into the milking process, it's essential to understand the anatomy of a goat's udder. The udder is divided into two halves, with each half having a teat. The teat is where the milk flows out, and it has a small opening called the teat orifice. Goats have small teats, so it's crucial to be gentle when milking them to avoid injuring the udder or causing discomfort to the goat.

One of the essential milking techniques is proper sanitation. Clean the udder and teats with warm water and a mild soap or a specialized udder wash before milking. This helps to remove any dirt or bacteria that can contaminate the milk. Dry the udder and teats with a clean towel before starting the milking process.

When milking, position the goat in a comfortable and secure place, such as a milking stand or a secure enclosure. It's essential to ensure that the goat is calm and relaxed as this can affect the milk let-down process. Begin milking by gently squeezing the teat at the base with your thumb and forefinger, using a smooth and consistent motion. Squeeze the teat rhythmically, alternating between the front and back teats, until the milk flow slows down or stops.

It's noteworthy that milking should never cause discomfort or pain to the goat. If you notice the goat becoming restless or uncomfortable, take a break and give her a chance to relax before continuing. You can also apply a small amount of udder balm or cream to the teats after milking to keep them healthy and prevent cracking or chapping.

As a goat owner, you should also be conversant with milking frequency. Most dairy goats should be milked twice a day, with a 12-hour interval between milkings. The milking schedule should be consistent to maintain the milk production level of the goat. In some cases, a third milking may be necessary, especially during peak lactation.

Milking equipment is another crucial factor in the milking process. Milking machines can be used for large-scale commercial operations, while hand milking is suitable for smaller-scale operations. The milking equipment should be properly cleaned and sanitized after each use to prevent the spread of bacteria and maintain the milk's quality.

Milk Storage and Handling

Milk storage and handling is an essential aspect of goat raising that requires proper attention and care to ensure that the milk is kept fresh and safe for consumption. Whether you are raising goats for dairy or meat, learning the right milk storage and handling techniques can help you maximize your yields and keep your goats healthy and productive.

One of the first things to consider when it comes to milk storage and handling is the cleanliness of the environment where the milk is produced. Milking equipment and surfaces should be cleaned and sanitized thoroughly before and after each milking session to prevent the growth of bacteria that can contaminate the milk.

To ensure that milk stays fresh and safe to drink, it is important to store it properly. The ideal temperature for storing goat milk is between 33 and 40 degrees Fahrenheit. Milk should be stored in a clean, airtight container made of food-grade material such as glass, stainless steel, or plastic. It is recommended to use a container specifically designed for milk storage, as it can help prevent the growth of bacteria and keep milk fresh for longer.

When storing milk, you need to keep it away from any strong-smelling foods such as onions or garlic, as these can affect the flavor of the milk. Milk should also be kept away from direct sunlight and heat sources, as exposure to these can cause it to spoil more quickly.

If you plan to transport milk, take necessary steps to keep it safe during transit. Milk should be kept in a cooler with ice packs or frozen gel packs to maintain a consistent temperature, avoid shaking or jostling the milk during transport, as this can cause it to separate and spoil.

Proper milk handling techniques can also help prevent contamination and ensure that milk remains safe for consumption. When milking goats, ensure you use clean hands and wear gloves to prevent the spread of bacteria. Milk should be filtered through a clean, food-grade filter before it is stored to remove any impurities or debris.

If you are planning to sell goat milk, it is important to follow local regulations and obtain any necessary permits or licenses. In some areas, selling raw milk may be prohibited or restricted, while in others, it may be required to have the milk tested for bacteria or other contaminants before it can be sold.

Making Goat Milk Products

When it comes to goat raising, one of the most rewarding aspects is making goat milk products. From cheese to soap, there are endless possibilities when it comes to utilizing goat milk.

The first step in making any goat milk product is, of course, milking the goats. It is vital to have a clean and sanitary environment when milking to avoid any contamination. The teats and udder should be cleaned before milking, and the milk should be immediately stored in a clean and sanitized container.

Once you have collected enough milk, it is time to start processing it into the desired product. One popular option is goat cheese. There are many different types of goat cheese, including soft cheeses like chevre and feta, and hard cheeses like cheddar and gouda. The process for making cheese can be quite involved, but it generally involves heating and curdling the milk, draining off the whey, and then pressing or aging the cheese to achieve the desired texture and flavor.

Another popular use for goat milk is in soap making. Goat milk soap is known for its moisturizing and nourishing properties, making it a popular choice for those with sensitive skin. To make goat milk soap, the milk is typically mixed with lye and other oils to create a smooth and creamy soap. The soap can then be scented and molded into bars for use.

Besides cheese and soap, there are many other goat milk products that can be made, including yogurt, ice cream, and even fudge. Each product requires its own unique process and ingredients, but with a little research and practice, anyone can learn to make their own delicious and unique goat milk products.

Of course, making goat milk products does require some equipment and supplies. For cheese making, you will need a cheese press, molds, and a thermometer. For soap making, you will need a scale, a mixing bowl, and soap molds. However, many of these items can be purchased relatively inexpensively, and once you have them, they can be used for years to come.

When it comes to selling goat milk products, there are some vital considerations to keep in mind. First and foremost, it is important to make sure that your products are safe and free from contamination. This means using clean and sanitary equipment, storing your products properly, and following any relevant food safety regulations.

It is also essential to market your products effectively. Make sure that your packaging is attractive and informative, and consider offering samples or discounts to help generate interest. Social media can be a great tool for reaching potential customers, as can farmers markets and other local events.

Overall, making goat milk products can be a fun and rewarding way to utilize your goat's milk. Whether you are making cheese, soap, or something else entirely, the possibilities are endless. With a little practice and some basic equipment, anyone can learn to make their own delicious and unique goat milk products.

CHAPTER 7

SELLING AND MARKETING GOAT PRODUCTS

Goat products can be a great way to diversify income for goat farmers and make the most of their investment. Selling and marketing goat products can be a profitable endeavor, as long as it is done correctly. This chapter will provide insight on selling and marketing goat products, including the types of products available, how to price them, and how to reach potential customers.

The types of goat products available range from cheese, to milk, to meat, to fiber. Each type of product has its own unique set of challenges and opportunities. Cheese, for example, requires specialized equipment and knowledge to produce and may be expensive for small farmers to produce in significant quantities. Milk requires a reliable milking system and the ability to keep the milk cold and safe until it reaches the consumer. Meat requires butchers and processors, as well as a reliable source of animals. Fiber products, such as wool and cashmere, require specialized equipment for shearing and processing.

In order to price goat products correctly, farmers must consider their costs and the market value of the products. A good way to do this is to conduct market research on the local and regional market, and compare the prices to the costs incurred by the farmer. Farmers should also consider factors such as the rarity of the product, the quality, and the distance the product must travel to reach the customer.

Marketing and selling goat products can be done in a variety of ways, depending on the budget and resources available. Traditional methods such as print and radio advertising, direct mail, and door-to-door sales can be effective, but may not be the most cost-effective option. Social media, online advertising, and word-of-mouth can also be effective ways to reach potential customers. Farmers can also consider selling at farmers' markets, partnering with local stores, or wholesaling their products to other businesses.

By taking the time to understand the market and the different types of products available, goat farmers can make the most of their business and create a successful venture. With the right pricing, marketing, and sales strategy, goat products can be a profitable venture for farmers.

Marketing Goat Meat and Milk

As a goat farmer, one of the most important aspects of raising goats is understanding the potential marketing opportunities for goat meat and milk. These products offer a unique opportunity for farmers to diversify their income streams and tap into growing markets that are increasingly interested in sustainably sourced and ethically raised products.

Goat meat, also known as chevon or cabrito, is a lean and flavorful meat that is widely consumed around the world. In recent years, it has gained popularity in the United States as a healthier and more sustainable alternative to beef and pork. This is due in part to its lower fat content, which makes it a great option for health-conscious consumers, as well as its lower environmental impact compared to other meats.

When it comes to marketing goat meat, focus on its unique characteristics and flavor profile. Unlike beef and pork, goat meat has a distinctively gamey flavor that can be enhanced with the right spices and cooking techniques. This can make it a great choice for adventurous foodies and home cooks who are looking to experiment with new flavors.

In addition to its taste, goat meat is also known for its versatility. It can be used in a wide variety of dishes, from curries and stews to tacos and kebabs. This means that there are many different ways to market goat meat to different audiences. For example, you might promote it as a gourmet ingredient for high-end restaurants, or as an affordable and healthy option for home cooks.

When marketing goat meat, it's also important to highlight its health benefits. Goat meat is low in fat and calories, high in protein, and contains vital nutrients like iron and vitamin B12. This makes it a great option for anyone looking to maintain a healthy and balanced diet. You might consider partnering with a nutritionist or health coach to promote the health benefits of goat meat to your customers.

Another main product to consider when marketing goats is goat milk. Goat milk is a nutritious and versatile product that can be used for a wide range of applications, from making cheese and yogurt to baking and cooking. Like goat meat, it has gained popularity in recent years as a healthier and more sustainable alternative to cow's milk.

When marketing goat milk, lay emphasis on its unique taste and nutritional properties. Goat milk has a slightly tangy flavor that can be a great option for people who find cow's milk too bland. It's also higher in protein and lower in lactose than cow's milk, making it a good choice for people with lactose intolerance.

To market goat milk successfully, you might consider partnering with local chefs and food producers to showcase its versatility. For example, you might work with a local cheesemaker to create a line of goat cheese products that can be sold in local stores and farmers markets. You might also partner with a local bakery to develop a line of baked goods made with goat milk.

When marketing goat meat and milk, you need to be transparent about your farming practices and animal welfare standards. Consumers are increasingly interested in knowing where their food comes from and how it was raised, so it's important to be upfront about your farming methods and any certifications or labels you have earned.

Finding Buyers

Marketing goat meat and milk can be a lucrative business, but finding buyers can be a challenge. In order to sell your products, you need to find people who are interested in buying them. Here are some tips for finding buyers for your goat meat and milk.

Identify Your Target Market

The first step in finding buyers for your goat meat and milk is to identify your target market. Who are the people who are most likely to buy your products? Are they health-conscious consumers looking for a lean protein source? Are they people with dietary restrictions who can't consume cow's milk? Once you have a clear understanding of your target market, you can tailor your marketing efforts to reach them.

Attend Farmers Markets

Farmers markets are a great place to sell your goat meat and milk. Not only do they provide a platform for you to showcase your products, but they also allow you to interact with potential customers and answer their questions. Additionally, farmers markets tend to attract people who are interested in buying locally produced, high-quality food products.

Partner with Local Restaurants and Chefs

Restaurants and chefs are always looking for unique and interesting ingredients to incorporate into their dishes. Reach out to local restaurants and chefs and offer to supply them with your goat meat and milk. You could even offer to provide them with a sample of your products so they can see the quality for themselves.

Utilize Social Media

Social media is a powerful tool for marketing your goat meat and milk. Create a social media page for your business and regularly post updates and photos of your products. You could even offer special promotions or discounts to your social media followers to incentivize them to purchase your products.

Advertise in Local Publications

Local publications such as newspapers and magazines can be a great way to reach potential customers. Consider placing an advertisement in a local publication that targets your target market. Make sure your advertisement highlights the benefits of your goat meat and milk, such as its high protein content or unique flavor.

Attend Local Events

Local events such as food festivals or fairs can be a great opportunity to showcase your goat meat and milk. Set up a booth at a local event and offer samples of your products. This will give people a chance to try your products and see the quality for themselves. Additionally, attending local events allows you to interact with potential customers and answer their questions.

Finding buyers for your goat meat and milk requires a combination of marketing efforts. Whether you attend farmers markets, partner with local restaurants, or advertise in local publications, the key is to get your products in front of people who are interested in buying them.

Building a Brand for Your Goat Farm

If you're starting a goat farm, you might not think that branding is a top priority. After all, it's easy to assume that your products will speak for themselves. However, in today's competitive market, a strong brand can make all the difference in the success of your business.

So, what does it take to build a brand for your goat farm? Here are some key steps to consider:

1. **Define your mission and values:** Your brand should reflect what your goat farm stands for. Consider your goals, your approach to farming, and what sets you apart from other goat farms. This will help you develop a brand that resonates with your customers.

2. **Choose a memorable name and logo:** Your farm's name and logo should be easy to remember and recognize. They should also reflect your mission and values. For example, if you prioritize sustainable and ethical farming practices, you might choose a name and logo that evoke nature and eco-friendliness.

3. **Develop a consistent visual identity:** Once you have a name and logo, you'll need to develop a consistent visual identity for your brand. This includes choosing colors, fonts, and imagery that align with your mission and values. Consistency is

key here, as it will help your brand stand out and be easily recognizable.

4. Build a website and social media presence: In today's digital age, it's essential to have a strong online presence. Build a website that showcases your products, tells your story, and allows customers to purchase your goods. Social media can also be a powerful tool for building your brand and engaging with customers.

5. Create high-quality products and packaging: Of course, your products themselves are a crucial part of your brand. Ensure that your goats are well-cared for, and that you produce high-quality milk, cheese, and other goat products. Pay attention to packaging, too – it should be visually appealing and reflective of your brand's identity.

6. Engage with customers and the community: Finally, building a strong brand is all about building relationships. Engage with your customers and the community in meaningful ways. Host events on your farm, attend local farmers' markets, and respond promptly and courteously to customer inquiries.

Building a brand for your goat farm takes time and effort, but it's well worth it in the end. A strong brand can help you stand out in a crowded market, build customer loyalty, and ultimately drive sales. By defining your mission and values, creating a memorable visual identity, producing high-quality products, and engaging with your customers and community, you can build a brand that sets your goat farm apart from the rest.

CHAPTER 8

TIPS FOR SUCCESSFUL GOAT RAISING

Congratulations on embarking on the journey of goat raising! Whether you're a hobbyist or a commercial farmer, raising goats can be a rewarding experience both financially and emotionally. However, like any livestock venture, it requires careful planning and attention to detail to ensure success. In this concluding chapter, we will look at some tips for successful goat raising that will help you achieve your goals as a goat rearer.

1. Choose the Right Breed:

Choosing the right breed of goats is critical to your success as a goat raiser. Not all goat breeds are created equal, and each breed has its unique characteristics that make them suitable for different purposes. Before you purchase any goats, research the various breeds available and determine which ones best fit your needs. For example, if you're looking for milk production, consider breeds like Saanen, Alpine, or Nubian goats. If you're interested in meat production, Boer goats are a popular choice.

2. Provide Adequate Housing:

Proper housing is essential to the health and well-being of your goats. Your goats need a clean, dry, and comfortable place to rest and escape from the elements. Consider the size of your herd, the climate in your area, and the type of housing that is suitable for your breed of goats. A sturdy fence around your property is also crucial to keep your goats from wandering off or being attacked by predators.

3. Provide Clean Water and Feed:

Goats require clean and fresh water at all times. Make sure you provide adequate water sources, especially during hot weather. Also, ensure that your goats have access to high-quality feed. Feed your goats a balanced diet that includes roughage, minerals, and vitamins. Providing your goats with good-quality hay, fresh pasture, and mineral supplements will help keep them healthy.

4. Practice Good Hygiene:

Goats are susceptible to various diseases, so practicing good hygiene is essential. Regularly clean and disinfect your goat's living quarters, equipment, and feeding and watering troughs. Additionally, practice good personal hygiene when handling your goats. Wear gloves and wash your hands regularly to prevent the spread of diseases.

5. Regularly Monitor Health and Behavior:

Regularly monitoring your goat's health and behavior is essential to identify any issues before they become significant problems. Observe your goats daily, looking for signs of illness, injury, or abnormal behavior. Early detection of any issues will allow you to take appropriate measures promptly.

6. Vaccinate Your Goats:

Vaccinations are crucial in preventing and controlling infectious diseases that can affect your goat's health. Consult with your veterinarian and develop a vaccination schedule for your herd. Vaccinate your goats against common diseases like tetanus, clostridium perfringens, and pneumonia.

7. Practice Proper Breeding:

Breeding your goats is an essential part of goat raising. Ensure that you have healthy and mature animals before you breed them. Consult with a veterinarian to ensure that your goats are in good reproductive health. Proper breeding will help you maintain the health and quality of your herd.

In conclusion, goat raising can be a rewarding experience when done right. Choose the right breed, provide adequate housing, feed, and water, practice good hygiene, monitor health and behavior, vaccinate your goats, and practice proper breeding. By following these tips for successful goat raising, you'll be well on your way to raising healthy and productive goats.

GLOSSARY

Biosecurity: Measures taken to prevent the introduction and spread of diseases in a goat herd.

Browsing: A method of feeding goats where they are allowed to graze and select their own food from a pasture or wooded area.

Buck: A male goat that has not been neutered.

Caprine: Relating to or belonging to the goat family.

Coccidiosis: A common intestinal disease in goats caused by protozoan parasites.

Colostrum: The first milk produced by a doe after giving birth, which is high in antibodies and essential nutrients for the kid.

Copper: A mineral essential for the health of goats, often included in their diet.

Dam: The mother goat of a kid.

Dehorning: The process of removing the horns from a goat.

Dipping: The process of immersing a goat in a solution to treat or prevent external

Estrus: The period of sexual receptivity in female goats, also known as "heat."

parasites.

FAMACHA: A system for checking anemia in goats, used to determine when they need deworming.

Fecundity: The ability of a doe to produce offspring.

Fleece: The wool or hair of a goat, which can be used for various textiles.

Foot rot: A bacterial infection that affects the hooves of goats, causing lameness and other symptoms.

Forage: The food that goats eat, including grass, hay, and other plants.

Gestation: The period of pregnancy in goats, which lasts around 5 months.

Goat cheese: Cheese made from goat's milk.

Goat milk: Milk produced by goats, which is often used for drinking, cooking, and cheese-making.

Hoof trimming: The process of trimming a goat's hooves to prevent overgrowth and other health problems.

Housing: The shelter and living space provided for goats, which should be clean, dry, and well-ventilated.

Immunization: The process of vaccinating goats to protect them from common diseases.

Inbreeding: The breeding of closely related goats, which can lead to genetic defects and health problems.

Johne's disease: A bacterial disease that can affect goats, causing diarrhea and other symptoms.

Kid: A baby goat.

Kidding: The process of giving birth to baby goats.

Lactation: The period during which a doe produces milk, usually lasting several months.

Mastitis: An inflammation of the udder in goats, which can be caused by infection or injury.

Meat goat: A breed of goat raised for meat production.

Milk stand: A device used to restrain a goat during milking.

Nubian: A breed of dairy goat known for its high milk production and distinctive long ears.

Offal: The internal organs and entrails of a goat, often used for food.

Parasites: Organisms that live on or inside goats and can cause disease or other health problems.

Pasture: A plot of land used for grazing goats.

Pygmy: A small breed of goat, often kept as a pet or for meat production.

Rangeland: A large, open area of land used for grazing goats.

Ration: The amount and type of food given to goats on a regular basis.

Sable: A breed of dairy goat known for its rich, creamy milk.

Scours: A diarrhea-like illness in goats, often caused by infection or poor diet.

Shelter: A protected area for goats to rest and seek refuge from the elements.

Show goat: A goat raised for competition in livestock shows.

Sire: The father goat of a kid.

Toggenburg: A breed of dairy goat known for its high milk production and distinctive coloration.

Udder: The mammary gland of a doe, used for producing milk.

Vaccination: The process of administering vaccines to goats to prevent common diseases and illnesses.

Wether: A castrated male goat, often kept as a pet or for meat production.

Worming: The process of deworming goats to prevent or treat internal parasites.

Yearling: A goat that is one year old but has not yet reached adulthood.

Zinc: A mineral essential for the health of goats, often included in their diet.